CW00839757

Sarah,

Hope you enjoy
the book,
Happy herb
growing

Louise
— x —

A witch with a difference

Wicca v Hedge
"coming together through herbs "

Dedication

To all my family and friends who believed what I had to say was worth listening to. My dad Neil Searle, who even though in ill health insisted on being my proofreader, my wonderful son Mathew Brack Bloomer who attended health & healing shows with me, smiling through gritted teeth, when I was doing talks and left him in charge of my stall; and my amazing loving husband Joe Bloomer, who has put up with me making phone calls in the middle of dinner or conversations, had idea after idea bounced off him, and had our lovely home taken over by bunches of herbs, crystals, decorated besoms and witchcraft paraphernalia of all descriptions, not to mention all the students who have trodden my floorboards over the years.

A special mention goes to both John Richardson - Hypnotherapist from the Feel better fast clinic and Joanne Csaczar - Spiritualist medium and Tea leaf reader, who both told me to just get on with it.

"A book stuck in your head, isn't a book!"

Of course I must mention all my amazing students but especially Sam and Beverley who have filled me with confidence with their kind words and kept the bank balance afloat with all the courses and stock they have purchased over the last two years. I can't thank you enough, you've both been truly amazing as have all the members of my Wiccan Lady group and many many other like minded people.

My last thank you goes to David Speight and his lovely wife Susan who run Morley Moot and encouraged me back out of my shell two and a half years ago after several personal and devastating things really knocked my confidence. Warm words and endless amounts of speakers not turning up to the moot, gave me the opportunity to get up and tell my story over several months and this became a healing process that I cannot thank them enough for giving me, what witch wouldn't want to talk to others about broomsticks, chakras, magical herbs, Wicca, hedgewitchery and their own personal path in witchcraft.

Illustrations of the flowers by Ms Sue Abbott of Kirkstall, Leeds.

Content

Forward

Like many people I didn't have the easiest of childhoods, my father was in the forces and we moved around frequently making it very hard to make true friendships, so throughout school all the forces children made friends quickly and parted even quicker, never to speak to each other again when families were posted away. This wasn't helped by the fact, I never really seemed to fit in, I was always the outsider and when I did make a friend it was usually the kid who was disliked even more than me. I used to take pity on what my mum called "the lame ducks".

I was brought up in the church, Church of England to be precise and used to attend family service and Sunday school, but the older I got the more I thought things just didn't add up. At sixteen I chose to be confirmed and the same vicar performed my marriage two years later, he was a padre and had an amazing way with people, but when we moved away, it took me a further twenty one years to find another vicar with the same qualities that sparked my interest. In the meantime, I had already bought my first pack of tarot cards and runes and started using them intuitively. I then started attending spiritualist church and that is when things began to fall into place.

My grandmother and nanna were both spiritual people, but living abroad for much of my childhood I didn't get to spend the time with them that I would have liked. My grandfather, whom I never met as he died before I was born would come and sit with me when I was upset and I always thought that was wonderful as we hadn't had a relationship in the physical world.

Walking down the street I would get messages for people pop into my head or other ancestors would come and sit with me, leaving their scent of perfume, tobacco or sherry in the room after they left, I was happy and felt like I was heading in the right direction, but there was something still missing; which now it turns out was nearly all of me - I started doing tarot parties to make additional money and friends would come round for coffee and ask me to do psychometry for them. I attended college and took qualifications in aromatherapy, reflexology, Indian head massage, Reiki and counselling, before learning other add ons like crystal healing and Hopi ear candling, each new course took me to a new place where I felt more at ease with being different to those around me.

In 2001 I started doing holistic fairs and shows, selling crystals and doing taster treatments and for a time I worked in a hotel spa in Leeds, but then a few years later Joe and I decided to start fostering and we learnt a whole new set of skills to help us welcome children from difficult backgrounds into our home.

It wasn't until I opened my own business again in 2010 that I came upon a young woman who was interested in my courses and she told me she was also a Wiccan and that she had been drawn to my shop by spirit because they knew I could help with her learning, I was really surprised as I didn't know anything about Wicca, I just knew I had witch like tendencies, loved herbs and believed that everything on Earth must have an opposite. The more I researched Wicca, the more I noticed the similarities in how I had been working, but then I would turn a page and think, I don't do that, that doesn't even make sense! I was totally confused; by putting a name to my craft, I was trying to shoehorn myself into very specific boxes and it really wasn't much fun.

In 2013 the friendship with this lady fell apart for no apparent reason and by then I had come upon the term hedgewitch, as I read more and more about it, again I thought , wow this is me, this is the path I'm living, with a few exceptions, all of which appeared to be Wiccan.

For the remainder of that year and the next, I researched both forms of witchcraft realising they were basically opposites. Wicca was ceremonial, ritualistic, calling on the God & Goddess in front of an altar. Where Hedgewitches had no need for an altar, celebrated for two days longer than Wiccans and placed a great emphasis on being in the garden, fresh air or woods, however, both loved herbs, which was also my passion, so over the following few years I learnt how to combine and use both forms of witchcraft, I didn't want to lose or leave behind either path and nor did my ancestors, who would come through to me while I was beating myself up about decisions I thought I needed to make and tell me to do what felt right, not what the books said.

On several occasions, talking to other people who called themselves witches, I was told I couldn't possibly be half hedgewitch and half wiccan, it just couldn't work, but the one thing I know for sure now is that Paganism is an umbrella and under that umbrella are lots of ribs that keep it in shape, those ribs represent many forms of witchcraft and other non Christian beliefs, meaning that not all witches or pagans will be walking the same path as you, but there is a silent agreement that "real witches" are accepting of all other pagan pathways. This is something to remember when people proclaiming to be witches have differing opinions to you and believe theirs is the only right opinion.

Wicca is an Earth religion which allows you to do as you want with the exception of causing harm to any other. You form a connection with the ancient Gods and Goddess for your magic work, hedgewitchery on the other hand is more what I would call the true witchcraft, taught and used by our ancient ancestors, when witches were in fact the village crone, midwife, healer, weaver and walker. By placing the two together, I can merge the old with the new, which is great, because at no point in my witchy life have I ever felt the need to cast a circle "skyclad" (naked), I have other warmer and more private ways of raising my magical energy for ritual work.

But that doesn't mean those who do wish to work skyclad are wrong, it would be a sad state of affairs if we were all the same, don't you think?

I wish I had been able to spend more time with my ancestors, I feel there was so much you could have taught me, my mum of course was also spiritual, in some respects too spiritual for her own good and it frightened her. On many occasions spirit would visit her only to be told to "get lost", or would pass through to say "goodbye" to her shortly after taking their dying breaths, and wondered what it would be like to on the receiving end of her shrieks of panic and diving under the quilt to pretend they weren't there.

On one occasion I was running a stall at an outdoor event and mum and dad came to visit. We were stood chatting when she burst into tears and total hysteria ascended, it turns out the event was on a field where a bloody battle had taken place in the 17th century. I'll never forget the fear on her face as she described the soldiers and bloodshed and the fact they wanted something from her that she felt unable to offer.

I decided then it was probably better to just get on with it on my own. She does occasionally come to me for spells of course!!

Chapter 1

Wicca v Hedge

Am I bothered that I am different? No, I'm not, I've got used to it and for the most part, quite enjoy the fact that I don't run with the crowd.

Years ago when I started teaching my students about witchcraft, the first thing I always said before we got started was "This is my path, this is my story, you are very welcome to share it and welcome to walk alongside me, but don't be surprised if not everything I say resonates with you, because you are you and I am me." I still hold that dear now. The point of learning something new is that you take it in, mash it around and investigate it further and wouldn't it be really boring if we all came to exactly the same conclusion? I have been on many courses and workshops and thought "I'm not sure I agree with that", but it doesn't mean that information is wrong, it just isn't right for me at this precise time that's all, there is a chance I will come back to that in the future and a chance I won't, but at least I know about it and can make a proper decision based on the information I was given, and that is what I expect my students to do, I don't want sheep, following my every move, I want somewhat like minded people who I can help, support and nurture and who can also give me new ideas to try, that is what education and learning is all about, no matter what your age, or the subject you are studying.

Following two totally different paths can be fun and also very confusing, sometimes when I get out of bed, my first consideration is which witch I am going to be that day.

The only way I can explain what a Wiccan-Hedge witch is, is by telling you I feel like an old fashioned witch, the village maiden, mother or crone, the midwife, the healer, but with more ground rules that suit my empathic nature.

So this is how I like to try and live, it is the basis of most of my decisions in life and of course I believe in Karma or the Rule of Three, which means what you put out there comes back to you threefold, whether positive or negative. Everything you put out into the Universe is like a boomerang, it eventually finds its way back to you and has picked up momentum along the way.

In effect I feel like I am the village witch; but with scruples, meaning no disrespect to hedgewitches who aren't wiccan, but I want to take responsibility for my own actions in the "here and now" and can't help but think how wonderful our World would be if we all took this on board, whether a witch, professor of science or sales person. If we have to take responsibility for our own actions from the moment we do or say something, I think more people would be inclined to "think first" and to live a better way of life. Doing any old thing that suits me and then asking the Goddess for forgiveness doesn't wash it in Wicca! But in hedgewitchery, anything goes, so to speak. We still do our best by the Earth and people, but if someone upsets a hedgewitch then it is gloves off and prepare to meet their wrath, the rule of three is not paramount and a hedgewitch will act first and hope for the best afterwards, or take the punishment on the chin.

Other obvious differences are how we celebrate the Sabbats, a hedgewitch has three days of enjoyment celebrating the day of, and both the day before and the day after, whereas Wiccans celebrate for one day only. Wiccans are very ceremonial and ritualistic, casting a circle, calling in the quarters and elements, the God and Goddess that they want to work with, but hedgewitches have no need for all the frippery associated with wiccan spell casting, a small corner in the garden or a quiet spot in the woods is their ideal choice for magic work because being a hedgewitch is about having a foot in both Worlds, the World we all know and live in and the other World where we hope to go after we depart our physical body, a World that spirit, the Fae and other Elementals reside in and to do this we only need our minds, an ability to meditate or to place ourselves into an altered state and maybe a flat stone to place a single candle on.

Wiccans on the other hand will have their full altar on display including statues of a Goddess, a besom, pentagram, incense sticks, crystals, athame, wand, chalice, dishes of salt and water to name but a few items.

The one thing that remains the same whatever type of witch you want to be, is that spell casting is about placing an intent out into the Universe, an intent that if it is done correctly should be specific and to the point. Casting a spell is like sitting in church and saying a prayer. You want something to happen and now you are asking for it from a source bigger than yourself.

Both wiccans and hedge witches are nature based and will often have jobs that are around medicine, therapies, ecology, animals, children and environmental or conservation positions. Empathy, healing and caring tend to be the basis for both witches.

When the Saxons invaded the British Isles in the 4th Century, they brought many forms of paganism with them, one being the haegtessa, which translated to English means 'hedge rider'. These witches communicated directly with spirit, they chose to get their information from source, hence 'riding the hedge', meaning to work in both worlds. Shamans are often regarded as a type of Hedge Witch, due to their ability to communicate with spirits at the highest levels. The Hedge Witch is usually considered as having a good plant knowledge and is drawn to medicine and healing, as well as being good at switching off and meditation. They can make themselves as one with nature when they need to work and take their path very seriously. Being a hedge witch is a way of life, not something you dip in and out of. It is also free flowing and non regimented, unlike Wicca. Hedge witches feel most at home surrounded by woods and trees, fields and meadows and love to sow and grow plants that support wildlife and can be used for cures for most ailments.

I was recently asked by someone on a well known social media platform "How do I become a witch?" and it really took me a while to consider my answer, which then looked like a thesaurus once I'd written it because there are two types of witch in my mind, the hereditary witch, who has come down the bloodline of their family, learning everything they need to know and how to achieve it through generations of trials and tribulations and then there are the other witches - The ones who over a space of time feel drawn to witchcraft and maybe don't even know why, maybe it feels strange to them, especially if up to this point they have followed another religion for instance. A witch is generally not something you wake up one morning and decide to become, it tends to be more accidental than that, although I am pretty sure there are no such things as accidents or coincidences, I believe that everything happens for a reason. Often the person may already be living a healing, nature filled and nurturing life, maybe they are learning tarot or mediumship, maybe they have just bought a new home with a garden and the thought of growing their own herb plot fills them with delight, but the one thing I 'feel' very much is that often these people have been witches in a previous life and the strong connections to the Earth and nature are again pulling through to this life.

I don't consider myself to be special in any way, but I noticed years ago that I have a 'special feeling' that I get when I am near witches who are on their second or more time around. I would get students coming to my courses or for tarot readings and I would feel a prickly slightly painful electric charge come about me, it didn't matter how well I had grounded and protected myself, it just happened and the more it happened, the more I took notice until it became a honed reaction to people. I would be in a room and someone would say, "I'm a witch" and my inner reaction straight away would be "oh, no you aren't" or people would say to me "I don't consider myself to be a witch, I just like herbs etc" and my prickly electric charge would be shooting out all over, I have now decided that many people who are resonating as a witch and don't realise it, maybe think being a witch is far more than it actually is, or that because they can't fly on a broomstick or get their basil and tarragon to blow up in a puff of green smoke it means they aren't a witch, but I've got news for you, there are far more of us out there than you would ever believe and that can only be a good thing.

Basically a witch isn't Harry Potter, Glinda the good witch, Maleficent or Meg and Mog, it's you and me and other perfectly normal looking people, both young and old, male and female.   So why not embrace it when it comes knocking at your door, you have no idea what wonders and delights might be in store for you.

Chapter 2

What you need to know about Wicca

A Wiccan can either be solitary or part of a coven, the choice is yours to make. Wicca has a very strong moral foundation despite it having solitary and coven lead practises.

Most Wiccans follow The Rede, a set of principles, guidelines or rules, however you wish to address it. The most important part being the original 8 words.

"An ye harm none, do as ye will"

Simply this means you can do whatever you feel like as long as you cause no harm to another, this goes as far as to include not just people, but also animals, plant based life and the Earth itself.

The Rede plays a large part in Wiccan practise. Some pagans believe it was written recently and in effect, it was; but many others believe the concept was taken from a far older origin.

Wicca is a very individual religion and yet many aspects are the same for all Wiccans. We respect nature and that includes other humans and animals and we seek to find a connection with the divine, which is usually in the form of the Goddess and God. Wicca is a polarity religion, we believe that everything has an opposite.

Some Wiccans see themselves as witches and some do not. Some believe that to be Wiccan you must be a witch, but not everybody has the same belief system and they may follow the Wiccan Rede but not be a witch. The choice is yours, but I will say I truly believe the two go hand in hand. Usually Wiccans who don't consider themselves to be witches believe so because they do not practise magic, which to most extent is what witches are thought to be about. They will worship the Goddess and God, celebrate the turning of the Wheel of the Year, and live at one with nature, but they have no reason to harness the natural energies of the Universe to help bring about desired changes in their lives.

It is interesting to note that the word "Wicca" comes from the Olde English for "sorcerer" or "diviner," and the Saxons used the word "Wicce" to mean "The wise". As the English language evolved, "wicce" eventually changed to "witch," this shift took place around the 1500s. It is known that Gerald Gardner referred to his coven members in and around the 1950/60's as "the Wica," and it is believed that this is where the modern name Wicca evolved from, not that Gerald Gardner invented Wicca, which many modern witches believe.

Most witches like myself, feel strongly that our history as a witch and self-identification as such, is being reclaimed from ancient times when witches were persecuted by most major religions. When being called a witch was a negative thing and accusational rather than a respected

title of a village Crone. Who wanted to be identified as a witch during the Burning times? Luckily, on the whole things are changing quickly and more and more people don't seem to bat an eyelid when I tell them I am a witch or teach witchcraft. The biggest issue I seem to have now is people asking me "Are you a white witch or you know, the other?" I am always tempted to make them say the words, "What do you mean, the other? What other?" If you are referring to a devil worshipper,
Pagans don't believe in the devil, that is a Christian concept. It is interesting to note that it is still against the law to be a witch in Saudi Arabia and Cameroon and that witch hunts still exist in parts of Africa and Asia.

I am neither a devil worshipper, a conjurer of green smoke or in the habit of placing small children in a cauldron, I do have two cauldrons though neither are for children!

In my Wiccan path, I believe there are two sides to everything such as, you cannot have day without night, cold without hot, male without female, good without evil and a god without a goddess, it is about two halves making a whole. As I mentioned before - polarity. I suppose an easy way to explain my thoughts are to go to the wheel of the year. It is round and ever turning, it passes through the stages of life - Maiden, Mother, Crone and also the stages of the year - Spring, Summer, Autumn and Winter and it covers the reproductive cycle of conception, birth, growth and death and the stage of the moon from dark to full. Apart from showing how everything is connected; we as humans, the seasons and even the moon, it represents a pattern that has never changed over thousands of years. We honor the life-giving and life-sustaining power of nature by creating rituals and committing to live in balance with the Earth, causing harm to none.

We celebrate the god during the turning of the wheel (Our calendar) and hold festivals to celebrate the Sabbats of which there are eight. These include four fire festivals - being Imbolc, Beltane, Lammas and Samhain, two Equinox being Ostara and Mabon and two Solstices being Litha and Yule.

The Goddess is then celebrated during the Esbats, which is the Full Moon rituals.

Taken together, all of these ritual celebrations comprise the Wheel of the Year, which Wiccans actively participate in "turning" as they mark the natural cycles of planting, growth, harvesting, and dying back. In this worldview, death is seen as an essential part of ongoing creation, as the old must make way for the new. The shadow side of life, represented by the "dark of the Moon" just before the Moon becomes new again, is every bit as important as the light. In this spirit, some forms of Wicca have a tradition of the "light half" and "dark half" of the year, marked by the Summer and Winter solstices, respectively.

Why is Wicca confusing - Well that is easy, although Wicca is predominantly a Pagan religion, there are also Christian Wiccans. Wiccans can also be witches, but aren't always and some people are witches and pagan but not Wiccan. Once you have got your head around this, it all seems so much easier!

I mentioned covens earlier, a coven is a group of like minded witches who meet for ritual work. A coven always used to be thirteen, which is the witch's number and also the number of goals a witch should try to adhere to. The coven is traditionally run by a High Priestess and High Priest, but some modern covens have no hierarchy and all members take it in turns to preside over the rituals. Members are usually initiated into the coven and the training for this will last a year and a day to show their commitment.

If of course you choose to be solitary and work on your own, you can self initiate through connecting with the Goddess, again there is usually a year and a day training programme before you would be ready to do this.

The best thing about Wicca is that there is no right or wrong to this type of witchcraft, if it feels acceptable to you and you can live with the consequences after considering the Threefold Law and the Wiccan Rede, then feel free to go for it.

So I see you looking a little dazed again, "Threefold Law" it isn't as strange as it sounds. This law is often called karma by others, Wiccans believe that what you put out into the World, comes back at you, meaning if you are horrible to someone, or curse them, or wish them ill, this negative energy will bound right back at you like a boomerang.

Negative energy has a habit of always finding its way home, so be careful what you wish for.

Threefold Law

Ever mind the rule of three,

What you put out returns to thee.

This lesson well, you should learn,

You only get what you earn.

The Wiccan Rede

Bide the Wiccan Laws we must In Perfect Love and Perfect Trust.

Live and let live. Fairly take and fairly give.

Cast the Circle thrice about to keep the evil spirits out.

To bind the spell every time let the spell be spake in rhyme.

Soft of eye and light of touch, Speak little, listen much.

Deosil go by the waxing moon, chanting out the Witches' Rune.

Widdershins go by the waning moon, chanting out the baneful rune.

When the Lady's moon is new, kiss the hand to her, times two.

When the moon rides at her peak, then your hearts desire seek.

Heed the North wind's mighty gale, lock the door and drop the sail.

When the wind comes from the South, love will kiss thee on the mouth.

When the wind blows from the West, departed souls will have no rest.

When the wind blows from the East, expect the new and set the feast.

Nine woods in the cauldron go, burn them fast and burn them slow.

Elder be the Lady's tree, burn it not or cursed you'll be.

When the Wheel begins to turn, let the Beltane fires burn.

When the Wheel has turned to Yule, light the log and the Horned One rules.

Heed ye flower, Bush and Tree, by the Lady, blessed be.

Where the rippling waters go, cast a stone and truth you'll know.

When ye have a true need, hearken not to others' greed.

With a fool no season spend, lest ye be counted as his friend.

Merry meet and merry part, bright the cheeks and warm the heart.

Mind the Threefold Law you should, three times bad and three times good.

When misfortune is enow, wear the blue star on thy brow.

True in love ever be, lest thy lover's false to thee.

Eight words the Wiccan Rede fulfill:

An ye harm none, do what ye will.

The rede takes a lot of digesting, but carries some very useful information that will help you on your path if you take the time to really understand it.

13 Goals of a Witch

1. Know Yourself
2. Know Your Craft
3. Learn
4. Apply Knowledge With Wisdom
5. Achieve Balance
6. Keep Your Thoughts in Good Order
7. Keep Your Words in Good Order
8. Celebrate Life
9. Attune With the Cycles of the Earth
10. Breathe and Eat Correctly
11. Exercise the Body
12. Meditate
13. Honor the Goddess and the God

Chapter 3

What you need to know about Hedge Witches

The term hedgewitch is ancient, the Saxons brought many ideas and concepts to the British isles and many of our witchcraft traditions stem from this. These beliefs mingled with the Celtic to create the "Craft" we have nowadays.

The word hedgewitch translates from the Saxon word "Haegtessa" which means hedge rider, the hedge as we know it today is something in the garden that divides two places, made of hawthorne, ivy, roses and shrubs, however in the Saxon term the meaning of a hedge was different, and related to forests and woods rather than a hedge made of plants. Forests were considered foreboding places that contained spirits and creatures like bats, spiders and wolves, and this made them frightening to most people. You can see this depicted in children's fairy tales and Hollywood movies.

Wise women and healers lived inside forests or just before the forest, it was therefore meant that they lived on the border of both Worlds, they lived in this dangerous World of the unknown and knew every plant and tree of the forest, yet they also lived in the physical realm, they were both in reality and the unknown World of magic, myth and mystery.

Many of us today think of ancient witchcraft being an old ugly woman with crooked bones living in a cottage by the woods on her own, with a house full of hanging herbs drying and withering, to make her potions. I may not live in a cottage or by the woods, but my house is full of herbs and many bunches of leaves and flowers, seeds and roots drying at any one time and I certainly don't consider myself "old".

As I've said before, witchcraft is nature based, so of course we love herbs and potions, lotions and tinctures, I believe it is fair to say that most people in the UK, if not much farther afield will have some connection to a witch of old, whether a distant relation or having bought or swapped something for a spell long before pharmaceutical companies took over our health regime. Witches or the village midwife, healer or weaver as you may like to call them were called upon by all sorts of people to provide help and answers to their situation, whether that was supporting a mother in childbirth, making an herbal charm to stop the spread of venereal disease or the pox or even to cause great pain and agony to a cheating husband's fancy woman. Their spell work was thought to be pretty much limitless, although done in secret to save themselves from persecution or worse.

Hedgewitches were predominantly women, single women, often by death or dissertation, a forest dweller who made spells and potions for healing. She was not evil but her practises were different compared to others.

No two hedgewitches are ever the same, individual by definition and they differ from any other practitioner of the Craft, hence why they are solitary people and true hedgewitches are never seen in covens, although they may occasionally get together to discuss magic and meditation.

One of the main ways they differ from Wiccan witches is that they do not conform to the Wiccan Rede, that is not to say that they do what they want when they want, far from it. Their moral compass is defined by the environment they work in; nature. Every hedgewitch has a certain set of morals and values which form their core and would never be broken if their life depended on it, and they are usually self governing.

They practice forms of natural magic, their spells are very simple and focus on intent and the Elements, they don't have set ceremonies, cast circles, invoke elements and deities as Wiccan witches do. The hedgewitch works with nature and the elementals instead, she is practical and will not have a need for a beautiful, fully tooled altar, she may not have an altar at all. She believes that magic comes from within, so has no need for utensils like a wand, athame or chalice. She works with her hands and with nature as everything she needs is within her, around her and flows through her.

Her knowledge of magical herbs, plants and trees is great, as she knows her environment like no other person and is acutely aware of the power and magic within every plant and knows their uses medicinally, magically and culinary. She is considered in modern day terms - an urban forager and her beliefs are closest to that of a medicine woman or Shaman. She is a healer, the herbalist of the community, but individuality and isolation is her preferred path. She is a trance worker who transcends many realms through her meditation.

Meditation gives us the ability to turn off our busy, mundane minds and reach out to connect with the spiritual world. It is in this "alpha state", that we are able to receive visions and messages from spirits and elementals, clear blockages in our chakras and energy fields, and travel to other realms on spiritual missions.

It is just as important to dream as it is to meditate and being able to remember your dreams is key. If you struggle with this then I suggest you buy a dream journal or notebook and start writing them down as soon as you wake in the morning. It doesn't have to be a biography, a few lines or little snippets will do. You should notice that after writing in the book for a while it becomes much easier to remember your dreams, even if you have several in one night. Dreams and meditation are connected, so if you can do one the other will come eventually. It is within our dreams we are also able to receive messages, recall past lives, travel to other realms, and heal.

Trance work is also a large part of being a hedgewitch and this is where the link to Shamanism comes in. A hedgewitch will learn the ability to put on shamanic drumming and switch into a trance like state. Years ago this was done with the use of hallucinogens, but I prefer to use legal ways to do it instead. The difference between a trance and meditation is that trance is deeper and allows you to go on a journey around Yggdrasil, the World Tree, as opposed to meditation which is mostly a state of relaxation. Some people can get into a trance state from their meditations, but I've never been very good at that! Try different ways until you find one that works for you, such as dancing barefoot, shamanic music, chanting, herbal drinks and potions containing mugwort, xhosa dream root or entada rheddi.

Anyone can bring hedgwitchery into their lives, even if they aren't a witch. Mindfulness which seems to be all the rage at the moment can help with this.

Many consider elementals to be mythical beings, but a hedgewitch would not hear of this. They believe that each element has elementals, such as Air being Sylphs, Earth being the Fae, Fire being Salamander and Water being Merpeople and during their trance-like meditations they will commune with the elementals, taking the information they are given from source.

Hedgewitches work with spirit, there is no getting away from this, it is as big a part of their religion as knowing how to heal. They enjoy their time in this liminal space - the space between the dead and the living Worlds and build their ability to communicate in different ways, not only through their trance work, but maybe through mediumship, the use of tarot or scrying, and tea leaf reading, the uses are unlimited.

It is believed that in medieval times that many hedgewitches could shapeshift and actually became animals and birds as a part of their work. Maybe this is where the idea of witches having a familiar came from? A familiar is an animal, mainly a pet nowadays like a cat, dog, rat or snake - that the witch was somehow connected with. The relationship is untouchable and witches today believe their familiars can help them in many ways, this is obviously true, as we hear lots of stories of dogs for instance alerting their owner if they need to eat due to a low blood sugar episode, or even opening the door if the owner is deaf and someone is knocking. Dogs to all intents and purposes are often as intelligent as their owners and will do mostly anything for a bowl of food and a loving home with cuddles. Toads, rats and mice, probably take a little longer to familiarise with. But I often talk to Fleur, my corn snake while I'm doing magic, or making a herbal brew for someone with an ailment, she is a good listener and never gives away my secret recipes.

Not everybody has the means or will to be a hedgewitch, which is why it is probably one of the lesser known and understood forms of witchcraft.
Hedge witches typically find magical intent in routine, day to day activities, hence why they are solitary people.

Shapeshifting

Hedgewitches have the ability to shapeshift as do Shamans, see that link keeps popping up. I'm not talking shapeshift as in turn into Spiderman or a werewolf of course.

I'm talking about a skill the Shamans have had dating back thousands of years, the same skill which was performed by witches for centuries.

During the Dark Ages, witches confessed to being shapeshifters in order to perform their magic.

Shapeshifting is also a way to journey into the other realms in disguise and protected from other beings who may do you harm. Even in Wicca, many Goddesses were shapeshifters, such as Aine, who took the form of a red mare, or the Morrigan who took the form of a raven and Elen of the Ways who changed into a reindeer.

It isn't an easy skill to master, but once you have there is on going back and changing into something else can be a very interesting experience.

Shapeshifting ultimately occurs while in dream state, astrally projecting, or in meditation and trance. Sometimes it happens naturally, without your willing it to and yet other times you will try and try and be unsuccessful, but like most things it is all down to practise and being in the right headspace.

If you want to try mastering this skill then why not go to bed holding a feather or a snake skin that has been shed, a piece of bone, or some other animal item. Start a meditation and focus on the energy, the life, and the soul of the animal that belongs to the item in your hand.

You literally want to get into the mind and body of the animal you want to shift into.

Forest Bathing

I find that forest bathing really helps in the practise of hedgewitchery and as we have already discussed, being in the woods and forests is where this form of witchcraft started centuries ago.

Use this method of being among the trees to connect fully with nature. By doing this you open yourself up to working with the fae and other elementals.

It is really important that you forest bath fully, so leave your mobile phone at home, yes I actually said it. I bet that has put a few of you off?

When you get to the entrance of the woods, slow yourself down, the idea is to notice everything. Take some long deep breaths, extending the exhalation of air to twice the length of the inhalation. This sends a message to the body that it should relax.

Stop and ask permission to be there. Listen for a rustle of leaves, the wind catching your cheek, any small sign that you are being made welcome.

Take a few moments to really listen to your surroundings, what can you hear? Animals, the wind, birds cheeping?

Consider what you are hearing in this space for the first time now that you are truly listening.

Now smell the air, depending what time of year it is there may be rotting leaves, new shoots, spring or summer flowers that attract the bees and butterflies to their nectar.

Take in your surroundings using all of your senses. How does the forest make you feel? Do you feel welcome, feel at home or feel like you shouldn't be there or you are being watched?

Just be in the moment and enjoy it. You may be surprised at the wildlife you see, but most of all while you are relaxed take note of any silver or gold flashing lights in the corner of your view. This means the fae are coming out to say hello and that is your first step to being a hedgewitch.

Don't forget to hug a tree or at the very least place your open palm on the trunk and thank the trees for letting you dwell in their space.

Chapter 4

Herbs in Witchcraft

Botanists and other scientific sources use a robust and specific set of characteristics to differentiate what is and isn't an herb from other types of plant form, but for witches, healers, weavers and even cooks, the term herb can include any plant that is useful to human or animal, whether being used for magical or mundane purposes.

Herbs, spices, woods and other plants, all of which will now be referred to as "herbs" in this book just to save time, have two main uses, the health properties and the magical properties. They of course help change the taste of food, dye our cloth, make furniture and so much more, but for the purpose of this book, we will concentrate on the magical uses mainly.

I know a lot about herbs used in magic, but I am not a herbalist and there is a huge difference. Some herbs as you will know, like Belladonna and Henbane are poisonous and look very much like other plants that have wonderful healing properties, so please be careful when picking from the hedgerow, you wouldn't go mushrooming unless you knew what you were doing would you?

Before you become connected with witchcraft would you have considered Sage as one of the most powerful herbs in your kitchen cupboard? That herb you buy in a small thin jar from the supermarket and drop a sprinkle into your bolognese sauce once a month? It helps boost immunity and fights infection, so is ideal for use in kitchen witchery, but magically Sage is used in spells and charm bags for immortality, longevity, wisdom and granting of wishes, most of us will use it for protection and it is seen burned in sage sticks for clearing and banishing negativity too.

Aristotle, the Greek philosopher believed that herbs had a psyche and Hippocrates studied medicine on the island of Kos with the use of herbs which he believed all had correspondence, such as a walnut looking like a brain and the oils in the nut being perfect for reducing the likelihood of a stroke and helping epilepsy amongst many other things.

Many Wiccan witches and hedgewitches would also agree that Aristotle and Hippocrates were correct in their beliefs and in fact, even scientists are now realising that plants actually have what we might define as consciousness.

Plants and trees have an amazing ability to communicate with each other, no matter where they live and they help each other to thrive, this can be seen especially well in forests and woods across the World. Discovering this helps us to see the inherent nurturing of Mother Earth and witches tap into this magical energy source when using herbs in their workings.

Poisonous herbs obviously cannot be consumed, but this doesn't mean they cannot be used. Charm bags and incense are a great way to include these toxic herbs, which often have very high magcal strength, but remember to wash your hands after handling them and keep them out of the reach of those who don't understand them. Children and animals can be very inquisitive and we all know what happens when you tell a child not to do something!! Always do your research too. The only safe way to use Belladonna is in incense form, the flowers and leaves mixed with other herbs like vervain, peppermint and thistle, makes a meditative trance incense, it isn't for me, but some do still use this as a means of astral projection too.

Herbs have been written about since people could write and there are also many drawings in caves showing plants used for healing or in ritual. Every herb has its own unique characteristics, making it special in its own right. Subsequently, this is why so many witches use herbs as part of their regular ritual practice. Abundance, healing, protection or hex breaking, there really is an herb for all occasions.

When using herbs in magic, remember that less is more. Each herb will have several areas it covers, so try not to mix more than three or four herbs together as this just confuses the mix. Pick your herbs depending on what you want the mix for, you wouldn't burn herbs in an incense that smells like rotten eggs for instance, or use Belladonna in an herbal tea or mouthwash, so choose accordingly.

When you have picked your three or four herbs, think about how you will infuse them with your magical intent, this is a very important stage of your magical workings. Throwing the herbs into a bag while considering what you're having for tea, isn't a very magical process and as you know by now, magical and spell work is all about intent, raising the energy and placing that intent into the universe to manifest.

Ideally you will be in a clean and tidy sacred space, you don't need an altar, but somewhere you go to be at peace, such as a spot in the garden or your kitchen, or the study, it is up to you. Then think about what you want to achieve, choose your tools and raise the energy around you. I hardly ever cast a circle, I'm too busy for that sort of thing, unless I'm calling in additional energies such as a goddess, ancestors or other spirits - then it is imperative. Instead I will either use reiki symbols, meditation, drum, sing the witches rune, clap my hands, burn candles and incense; the ideas are endless and it really is whatever feels right for you at the time and on that day.
When I feel ready, I then start my magical workings, if that includes saying a spell, I chant the words with meaning and passion, imagining the outcome I am looking for. For instance if your spell is to heal a leg ulcer, you imagine a fully fixed leg, looking gorgeous, not the ulcerated leg with the sores on it. "What you want to happen - not what is".

If you are mixing herbs, but not saying anything, for a charm bag for example, then while you mix the herbs together think about the outcome. Often I will repeat a single word while I do this, like "healing" or "protection", and I always mix the herbs with my index finger on my power hand (predominant hand). Imagine white or purple light coming from the end of your index finger and blending the herbs together in magic, if that helps. Some people mix with their wand or a special spoon.

You may want to use herbs that correspond to particular Elements, especially if you work with the horoscopes such as Gemini being an Air sign and to make this easier I have added the elemental signs to all the herbs in the grimoire.

Don't over complicate things, have fun, but be professional when using herb magic. It really should be enjoyable, just don't forget it is also work and can be very dangerous if left in the wrong hands.

I really hope you enjoy the Grimoire.

Herbal Grimoire

Acorn - Good luck, personal power, protection and wisdom. Dried acorns are a natural amulet for youthfulness. Associated with Litha. Element water.

Agrimony - Shielding and hex-breaking, aids sleep, brings luck towards you and is powerful in spell reversal. Element Air.

Alder - Helps you to face up to things you are avoiding, divination, teaching especially anything arty and weather magic. Element Fire.

Alfalfa - Money, prosperity and a happy home, also anti-hunger. Generosity and luck. Element Earth.

Allspice - Draws money and business success. Aids compassion, luck and healing. Element Fire.

Angelica - Also called Archangel. It is a very powerful protection herb, healing, creates harmony and courage and helps in exorcisms. Aids vision. Element Air.

Apple - Garden magic, love, healing and wisdom, also vanity, marriage and beauty. Associated with Mabon & Samhain. Element water.

Ash - Spells relating to the sea, protection, and luck. Make your Yule log from ash and burn to bring prosperity. Yggdrasil was an Ash tree. Element water.

Basil - Also called witches herb. Use in spells for Love, exorcism, wealth, sympathy, and protection. Associated with Imbolc. Aids astral projection. Element Fire.

Bay Leaf - Protection, success, purification, strength, wisdom and healing, also increases psychic powers. Element Fire.

Beech - Happiness, inspiration and divination. Represents the Green Man. Element Air.

Belladonna - Also Called: Deadly Nightshade. Toxic. Use for forgetting past loves. Protection, beauty and original flying ointments. Adds energy to rituals. Element Water.

Benzoin - Purification, prosperity, and helps to soothe tension by dispelling anger and lessening irritability, de stressing, helps depression, concentration and astral projection. Element Air.

Bergamot - Money, prosperity and sleep. Protects from both evil and illness. Good for luck and wealth. Increases magical power. Element Fire.

Birch - Protection, exorcism and purification. Dispels lightning, infertility, and the evil eye. Associated with Yule. Element Water.

Black Pepper - Banishing negativity, exorcism, and offers protection and help with inner strength. Element Fire

Blackthorn - Exorcisms, warding off negative spirits and general protection. Associated with Samhain. Element Earth.

Bladderwrack - Protection, sea and wind spells, attracts money, psychic powers, and customers to your business. Element Water.

Blessed Thistle - or Holy Thistle. Purification, protection against negativity and evil, hex breaking and aids vitality. Carry on you for strength and protection. Element Earth.

Borage

Blueberry - Protection of children, keeps evil out, and strengthens the aura. Associated with the Great Spirit. Element Water.

Borage - Courage, strength and peace, plus aids psychic powers. Also ward's off evil. Calming and de-stressing. Element Air.

Burdock - Also called Beggar's buttons. Used for cleansing magic and warding off negativity. Protection, healing and persistence spells. Element Earth.

Calendula - Also called Marigold. Attracts success and justice in legal matters. Increases psychic/spiritual powers and aid prophetic dreams. Dispels negativity. Element Fire.

Cardamom - Lust, love, and fidelity. Sweetens the personality Use in handfastings. Element Water.

Carnation - Protection, strength, healing, enhancing magical powers, and achieving balance. Element Fire.

Catnip - Also called Nepeta. Use when working with animals. Draws love, luck and happiness, also used in beauty magic. Associated with Bast. Element Water.

Cedarwood - Luck, strength and power. Helps increase money and protection. Also healing.   Associated with Mabon. Element Earth.

Cedar Berries - Also Called: Juniper Berries. Protective, cleansing and repels negativity very well. Used in healing rites. Element Fire.

Celandine - Cures depression, treats piles, improves circulation. Brings about Joy and happiness. Solar Magic. Element Fire.

Chamomile - Love, sleep, protection and purification, also reduce stress. Use for meditation work and to attract money. Solar Magic. Element Water.

Chervil - Helps healing, flatulence and superstition. Is considered the herb for bringing in new life. Element Water.

Chickweed - Also called Witches Grass. Use in moon spells. Also good for animal magic, relationships, love and fertility. Element Water.

Chili - Fidelity, love and passion. Also hex breaking. Element Fire.

Cinnamon - Also called Sweet Wood. Use for Solar magic. Meditation and astral projection. Increases spirituality, success, healing, protection, power, luck, strength, and prosperity. Element Fire.

Clover, Red - Also called Trefoil. used in any spells relating to marriage, love, lust and fidelity. Aids success linked to money also. Element Air.

Clove - Use to protect, banish negative forces, and divination. Also helps with any teeth spells. Aids money and draws love. Element Fire.

Coltsfoot - Aids wealth. Works with peace, tranquility, prosperity, and love. Associated with Brighid. Element Water.

Comfrey - Also called Slippery Root. Supports magic healing and safe travel. Use for money, endurance and stability spells. Element Water.

Coriander - Love, lust and health. Used as an aphrodisiac and to heal migraines. Brings peace & protection to the home. Element Fire.

Cornflower - Used primarily as an Ink for your Book of Shadows. It is the patron herb of herbalists. Use in rituals to give honor to the Mother of all nature, also connected to Rainbow and Crystal children. Element Earth.

Cumin - Fidelity, protection, and exorcism. Also used in love spells and food which can also promote fidelity. Element Earth

Cypress - Associated with death and mourning; stimulates healing and helps overcome the pain of loss. Other properties include self esteem, protection, love and banishing nightmares. Element Earth.

Damiana - Lust, sex magic and attracting love. It is thought to be an aphrodisiac. Use for astral projection and spirit quests. Element Fire.

Dandelion Leaf - Used to summon spirits, make wishes on, healing, purification and defeating negativity. Element Air.

Dandelion Root - Magical uses include divination, wishes and calling spirits. It also enhances dreams and works well in astral projection. Element Air.

Dock Root- **(Yellow).** Used to release baggage no longer needed. Also fertility, healing and money magic. Clears blockages and cuts bindings. Solar Magic. Element Air.

Echinacea - Adds a boost to clairvoyant and psychic abilities. Adds powerful strength to spells used in money drawing magic, fertility and abundance and provides the user with protective power. Element Earth.

Elder Tree - Sleep, releasing enchantments, protection against negativity, banishing. Element Water

Elderflower & **Berry** - Peace, protection, and healing, plus aids in exorcisms. Element Water.

Elm - Energises the mind and balances the heart. Aids love spells, and offers protection from lightning. Element Water.

Evening Primrose - Use in moon magic, love charms and to attract fae. Element Water.

Eyebright

Eyebright - Increases mental power, psychic ability and inner vision. Element Air.

Fennel Seed - Helps with meditation. Healing, purifying and protection. Also linked with new motherhood and offers inner strength. Element Air.

Feverfew - Aids poor health. Protection against accidents when travelling and protection when working with spirit. Carry on you for inner strength. Element Water.

Flax Seed - Also called Linseed. Used for money spells and healing rituals. Helps with beauty spells and offers protection. Element Fire.

Frankincense Resin - Use in solar magic. Associated with Beltane, Lammas, and Yule. Use in rituals and magic associated with self-control, spirituality and protection. Also regulates emotions and helps depression. Element Earth

Fumitory - Associated with the underworld and used at Samhain. Linked to spells for monetary gain, consecration and protection. Element Earth.

Galangal Root - Also called Lo John the Conqueror or Lo John. Carry into legal proceedings to help win. Money, gambling and hex breaking. Also aids luck and psychic development. Element Fire.

Garlic - Magical uses include speed, health and endurance, also protection, exorcism and purification. Use also to promote your inner strength. Element Fire.

Gentian - Increases spell power. Good luck and works well in love & romance spells. Element Fire.

Ginger - Increases magic power. Success, love, money and power. Element Fire.

Ginseng - Promotes love, beauty, healing and lust. Element Fire.

Hawthorn Wood- Associated with Beltane. Magical uses include chastity, fertility, fairy magic, fishing magic, and rebirth. Success in career, work, and employment. Use it to work with the fae. Used in weddings and handfastings to increase fertility. Element Water. Hawthorne Berries aid chastity. Hope, protection and happiness. Element Fire.

Hearts Ease - Also called Violet. Helps to mend a broken heart. Aids rebirth, peace, wishes and luck. Calms the nerves and promotes peace and tranquility. Element Water.

Hemlock - Use to paralyze a situation and a funeral herb. Highly Toxic. Element Water.

Henbane - Dried leaves are used in the consecration of ceremonial vessels. Used in love sachets and charms to gain the love of the person desired. Highly Toxic. Element Water.

Hibiscus - Attracting love and lust. Use in divination. Associated with lunar magic. Element Water.

High John - (The Conqueror) An "all purpose" herb. Use for strength, confidence, conquering any situation. Good luck, prosperity and protection. Element Fire.

Horehound - Protective against evil doings. Helps with mental clarity during ritual; stimulates creativity/inspiration; balances personal energies and healing. Element Earth.

Horsetail - Use for strength and resolve. Protection, cleansing and clearing unwanted emotions. Element Earth.

Hyssop - Used for purification. Banishing, protection and healing. Element Fire.

Irish Moss - Used for luck. Ideal for gamblers! Attracts money and customers for self employed. Offers protection. Element Water

Ivy - Protection, healing and fertility. Use for love and hang at handfastings. Element Fire.

Jasmine - The herb of attraction. Helps prophetic dreaming, money and love. Element Water.

Juniper - See Cedarberries.

Lady's Mantle - Aphrodisiac and transmutation. Use in love spells and those of fertility. Increases magic power in spells and connects with fairy lore. Element Water.

Lavender - Magical uses include healing, sleep and peace. It also promotes chastity and love. Increases longevity of life, tranquility and happiness. Element Air.

Lemon Balm - Also called Melissa. Love, success and healing. Aids psychic/spiritual development. Supports mental health disorders and compassion. Element Water.

Lemon Grass - Psychic cleansing and opening. Use in lust potions and when using Dragon Magic. Element Air.

Licorice Root - Love, lust, and fidelity. Also attracts passion. Element Water.

Lilac - Wisdom, memory, good luck and spiritual aid. Element Water.

Lime Tree Leaf - Healing, calm and love. Aids strength and tranquility, Element Air.

Little John - See Galangal root.

Lungwort

Lungwort - Use in air magic or as an offering to the Gods of air. Offers safe travel when flying. Element Air.

Mandrake - Spell strengthening. Use for protection, happiness and wealth. It aids money multiplying. Element Earth.

Marigold - See Calendula.

Marjoram - Use for cleansing, purification, and dispelling negativity. Also aids grief and sadness. Element Air.

Marshmallow Root - Protection and psychic powers. Use in tea to aid sore throats. Handfasting herb and cleansing. Element Water.

Meadowsweet - Used to increase the chances of getting a job. Helps peace, love and happiness. Aids divination. Element Air.

Mint - Promotes energy, communication and vitality, protection and draws custom. Element Air.

Mistletoe - Also called Witches Broom. Used for fertility, creativity, and protection from negative spells & magic. Hang at handfasting to kiss beneath and promote peace. Element Air.

Mountain Ash Berry - Also called Rowan Berry. Strong fairy and Goddess connections. Aids protection and meditation, helps to clear the mind. Element Fire.

Mugwort - Use for strength, protection and healing. Mugwort amplifies magic. Aids astral projection, and psychic power. Element Earth.

Mullein - Represents the cross roads. Offers protection from nightmares & hexing. Attracts love and keeps evil energies and spirits at bay. Element Fire.

Mustard Seed - Courage, faith, and endurance. It is a good luck amulet. Aids mental power and offers protection. Element Fire.

Myrrh - Spiritual, meditation, and healing. Supports youthfulness and protection. Luck and peace. Element Earth.

Nasturtium - Banishing and releasing fear. Helps create your own reality. Aids creativity and independence. Element Air.

Nettle - Uses include dispelling darkness & fear,and curse breaking. Healing and protection and increases lust in partners. Renewal. Element Fire.

Nutmeg - Magical uses include attracting money/prosperity, and luck. Use for fortune telling and when you need favourable decisions to be made. Element Fire.

Oak - Connected to Litha and the most sacred of all trees. Oak supports success, good luck and healing. Stability and potency and attracts money. Element Water.

Orange Peel & Flower- Attracts abundance, luck. Love and happiness and strengthens divination. Element Fire.

Oregano - Aids astral projection, health, and vitality. Increase joy and justice and protects against evil. Use at Handfastings. Element Air.

Paprika - Use this herb to help break hexes or bad luck. Increased love and passion. Increases energy and boosts magic. Element Fire.

Parsley - Use this herb to help with contacting the dead. Increases strength, vitality and passion. It is uplifting and helps spiritual growth. Element Air.

Passion Flower - Attracts friendship and passion. Calming, peace and instills passion into stale relationships. Good for house blessings too. Element Water.

Patchouli - Used in spells for connecting with spirits. Attracts money, increases fertility and lust. Calming and peaceful. Element Earth.

Penny Royal

Pennyroyal - Use for peace, harmony and tranquility. Carry to avoid seasickness or for physical strength & endurance. Element Earth.

Peppermint - Use for headaches and other forms of healing. Increases sleep and love. Use for increasing psychic power and divination. Element Air.

Pine/Needles - Prosperity and success. Protection, purification and divination. Throw in the fire to dispel negativity. Use in house and business blessings. Element Fire.

Plantain - Increases fertility and libido. Healing, protective and offers strength. Use to have power over supernatural events. Element Earth.

Poppy Seeds - Pleasure, love and luck. Aids sleep and insomnia. Use in astral projection and flying magic. Increases fertility and happiness. Element Water.

Pumpkin Seed - Use in lunar magic to honour the moon. Also healing and increases divination. Element Fire.

Raspberry Leaf - Used for healing, protection, love. Raspberry leaf not to be eaten by pregnant women until the due date, as it induces labour. Helps to reduce the pain involved in childbirth. Supports sleep, dreams and love. Element Water.

Red Clover - Aids success, love and money. Increases fidelity. Use in exorcism. Element Air.

Rose - Use for divination, increased psychic power, love, lust and healing. Helps strengthen close friendships. Place around sprains and bruises to help them heal faster. Element Water.

Rose Hips - Used in healing spells or to bring good luck and invoking good spirits. Aids stronger love. Element Water.

Rosemary - Use in healing poppets and love/lust spells. Improves memory. Increases sleep, mental power and protection. Burn to help purification and removing negativity. Associated with faery magic. Element Fire.

Rowan - See Mountain Ash.

Rue - Use in healing, health and love. Also, protection against the evil eye. Increases mental power and clarity of the mind. Used in exorcism. Element Fire.

Sage - Used for self purification and cleansing. Helps grief and loss. Healing and protection, also increases wisdom. Element Air.

Sandalwood - Burn during protection, healing, and exorcism spells. Aids luck and success, meditation and divination. Raises a high spiritual vibration. Element Water.

Skullcap - Aids love, fidelity and peace. Increases harmony. Element Water.

Sea Salt - Use to cleanse crystals and tools. For purification, grounding and protection. Supports ritual work. Absorbs negativity and banishes evil. Element Earth & Water.

Sheep Sorrel - Carry to protect against heart disease. Cleansing and increasing luck. Use in faery magic. Element Earth.

St. John's Wort - Worn to prevent colds & fevers. Induces prophetic and romantic dreams. Protects against hexes and black witchcraft. Increases happiness. Use in Solar Magic. Element Fire.

Star Anise - Consecration, purification, and happiness. Use for curse breaking or increasing luck. Burn to increase psychic awareness. Element Fire.

Strawberry Leaf - Attracts success, good fortune, and favorable circumstances. Increases love and aids pregnancy. Element Water.

Sunflower - Energy, protection, and power. Aids wisdom and brings about wishes. Use in fertility magic. Element Fire.

Sweet Cicely - Use during rituals for the dead or dying. Helps with divination and the contact of spirit. It is sacred to the Goddesses of death. Element Earth.

Sweetwood - See Cinnamon.

Tansy - See Agrimony.

Tarragon - Increases self confidence. Use in Dragon magic. Aids healing after abusive situations. Element Fire.

Tea Leaves - Use for courage or strength. In tea for increasing lust. Burn leaves to ensure future riches. Element Air.

Thistle - See Blessed Thistle.

Thistle

Thyme - Attracts loyalty, affection, and love. Increases good luck and psychic power. Drink in tea to aid sleep. Element Air.

Valerian - Also called Graveyard dust. Aids sleep, is calming and a sedative. Quietens emotions. Supports protection and love. Element Water.

Vervain - Strengthen others herbs. Helps, peace, love and happiness. Burn the leaves to attract wealth and keep your youth. Increases chastity also. Element Water.

Verbena - Psychic protection, peace and purification. Healing, and helps depression. Increases beauty and love. Mind opening and clearing. Ideal use for exams. Element Earth.

Violet - See Heart's Ease.

White Willow Bark - Use in lunar magic. Reduces negativity and removes evil forces and hexes. Use in healing spells. (Aspirin). Place dried pieces of bark in the gum when you have toothache. Element Water.

Willow - Used for lunar magic, drawing or strengthening love, healing, and overcoming sadness. Element Water.

Witches Grass - Happiness, lust, love, and exorcism. Reverses hexes. Element Earth.

Wood Betony - Use for purification, protection, and the expulsion of evil spirits and nightmares. Draws love in your direction. Element Fire.

Woodruff - Use to attract money, abundance and prosperity. Helps win victory especially for athletes. Element Air.

Wormwood - Used to remove anger, stop war, inhibit violent acts, and for protection. Use in clairvoyance, to summon spirits, or to enhance divinatory abilities. Element Earth.

Yarrow - Healing, calming and increases love. Used in handfasting & weddings. Increases psychic power and divination. Gives courage when needed. Element Air.

Herbs by Topic

Use this if you want to go straight to an herb for a specific issue you need to deal with. It also shows you herbs you can mix together to strengthen your magic in that area.

Calling Spells	Calming & Peace	Cleansing & Purification
Dandelion Leaf	Colt's Foot	Birch
Devil's Claw	Borage	Bladderwrack
Gentian Root	Elderflower	Chamomile
Lady's Mantle	Elderberry	Fennel
Patchouli	Heart's Ease	Horsetails
Sweetwood	Patchouli	Hyssop
Wormwood	Peppermint	Marshmallow
Witches Grass	Penny Royal	Plantain
	Valerian	Sage
	White Willow	

Divination & Vision	Exorcism	Faery Magic
Angelica	Angelica	Evening Primrose
Damiana	Birch	Hawthorn
Dandelion Leaf	Cumin	Horsetail
Devil's Claw	Elderflower	Lady's Mantle
Gentian Root	Fennel	Rowan Berry
Hibiscus	Hibiscus	Sheep Sorrel
Meadowsweet	Horehound	Witches Grass
Mugwort	Lungwort	
Parsley	Mandrake	

Fertility	Handfastings	Happiness & Tranquility
Hawthorn Leaf or Berry	Cardamom	Celandine
Horsetail	Clover	Colt's Foot
Lady's Mantle	Hawthorn	Hawthorn Berry
Licorice Root	Ivy	Hawthorn Leaf
Marshmallow	Marshmallow	Horsetail
Patchouli	Mistletoe	Lavender
Poppy	Yarrow	Meadowsweet
Strawberry Leaf		Nepeta
Witches Broom		Poppy
Witches Grass		St John's Wort

Healing & Health	Hex & Curse Breaking	Loss & Grief
Archange	Agrimony	Hawthorne
Ash Leaf	Cumin	Linden Flower
Blessed Thistle	Horsetail	Marjoram
Burdock	Hyssop	Motherwort
Coriander	Lungwort	Rose
Elderberry	Mandrake	Sage
Feverfew	Mullein	
Holy Thistle	Nepeta	
Hyssop	Nettle	
Melissa	Penny Royal	
Nettle	Plantain	
Tansy	Red Clover	
Witches Broom	St. John's Wort	

Love & Lust	Luck & Success	Lunar Moon Magic
Cardamom	Acorn	Evening Primrose
Chamomile	Galangal	Gentian Root
Coriander	Linseed	Hibiscus
Damiana	Heart's Ease	Lady's Mantle
Heart's Ease	High John	Pumpkin Seed
Hibiscus	Irish Moss	Witches Grass
High John	Mandrake	White Willow
Licorice Root	Marigold	
Lime Tree Leaf	Melissa	
Marshmallow	Poppy	
Mullein	Strawberry Leaf	
Nepeta	Sweetwood	
Witches Broom	Witches Herb	

Meditation	Money & Prosperity	Peace
Dandelion Leaf	Basil	Chamomile
Jasmine	Bay	Lavender
Lavender Melissa	Cinnamon	Meadowsweet
Mountain Ash	Mandrake Poppy	Peppermint
Slippery Root	Slippery Root	Raspberry Leaf
Valerian	Witches Herb	Tansy
		Valerian
		Witches Grass

Prophetic Dreams	Protection	Psychic Power
Chamomile	Angelica	Bay
Damiana	Ash Leaf	Bladderwrack
Dandelion Leaf	Bladderwrack	Devil's Claw
Jasmine	Beggars Buttons	Eyebright
Marigold	Cumin	Galangal
Raspberry Leaf	Elderflower	Mugwort
	Elderberry	Parsley
	Fennel	Patchouli
	Feverfew	Peppermint
	Linseed	Penny Royal
	Horehound	Plantain
	Irish Moss	Sage
	Lime Tree Leaf	Sweetwood
	Nettle	Yarrow
	Parsley	
	Sage	
	White Willow	

Sleep	Solar & Sun Magic	Spiritual Growth
Agrimony	Celandine	Dandelion Leaf
Chamomile	Cinnamon	Galangal
Lavender	Chamomile	Horehound
Meadowsweet	Frankincense St	Lady's Mantle
Peppermint	John's Wort	Mugwort
Raspberry Leaf	Yellow Dock Root	Parsley
Tansy		Sage
Valerian		Sweetwood
Witches Grass		White Willow
		Wormwood

Strength	Strengthening Spells	Wisdom
Angelica	Bergamot	Acorn
Bay	Carnation	Bay
Thistle	Echinacea	Gentian Root
Borage	Galangal	Horehound
Fennel	High John	Lady's Mantle
Feverfew	Holy Thistle	Sage
Holy Thistle	Lady's Mantle	
Mugwort	Mugwort	
Red Clover	Pumpkin Seed	
Rue	Rue	
	Wormwood	

Using Herbs

It is always best to try and grow your own herbs where possible and you don't need a big space to do it either. Many herbs can be grown on a windowsill or in planters on a balcony if you don't have a garden.

The time to gather depends on the type of plant, but the general rule of thumb - Bark in the spring, Leaves before the plant flowers, flowers on the first day they open and roots in the autumn. Try to collect in the morning when the sun has dried the dew but before the heat of the day. Use a sharp knife to cut the herbs, ideally it should be consecrated for this job. Only take as much as you need, unless pruning the plant for its next season.

Harvesting can be done a few ways, picking the tops of the plant, collecting seeds, gathering from the ground (nuts), cutting or pulling. Only the best shaped and coloured leafs should be picked. When a whole plant is harvested the leaves closest to the root will usually be imperfect so cut these away with a sharp knife or secateurs. Pulling the leaves or flowers off stems can lead to damage to the plant, causing a route in for fungus or bugs which will delay new growth or kill the plant.

A plant need not be destroyed even when the roots are what is required, take a small root cutting to re plant. Dig out the root of a plant when the leaves begin to die back, this needs to be done with a spade or fork to ensure no damage to the root. Perennials shouldn't have more than a third of their growth removed at any one time.

When drying the herbs, dry leaves on the stem so they don't get bruised, it makes it much easier to hang them too. Tie the herbs by their stems in small bunches and allow to dry in natural heat. Don't over bunch as they need air to circulate around them to stop them going mouldy. Remember to label the plants if drying more than 1 herb at a time, an easy way to do this is to write on a sticky label and attach this to the string/twine or cotton.

Leave for about three to six weeks to dry thoroughly depending on the water content. If the leaves crack when you pinch them, they are ready. Once dried herbs can last two to four years if stored properly but this does depend on the type of plant you are working with. Flowers and leaves will waste quicker than roots and seeds and those with high volatile oils such as chamomile and peppermint will waste quicker than those without such as plantain.

Chapter 5

Considerations

We need to consider which herbs we might use for what? Especially as some herbs cover many different subjects. This may be made easier if you only grow a few varieties in your garden or have specific herbs you like to work with.

It is also important to be clear about your intentions for the spell, ie if you want a love spell - do you need to: a. find a new love, b. fidelity, c. rekindle the passion in an existing relationship or d. improve your friendships. Hence why being specific is important.

You are not restricted to using one herb as many herbs go well together or help incorporate additional parts to the spell, ginger for example is good to use if you want the spell to work quickly and mugwort to strengthen the spell. But recall previously in the book where I stated, don't go daft and mix everything you have, try to stick to three or four maximum. Once you are sure about what you want to achieve you can make a list of possible herbs, excluding those that are impractical to get hold of. Then plan how you are going to use the herbs, obviously you don't want to make a tincture or tea bag from a toxic herb, but a charm bag or poppet would be okay.

Also think about what grows at what time of year, if you don't have it in the garden, where can you source the herb you need, that is practical and where your own moral compass is met?

I stock around one hundred and sixty herbs, spices, flowers and barks, but there are many many more you could work with, so start looking for reputable sources as soon as you can.

www.thewiccanlady.co.uk/herbal-grimoire

Magic with herbs

Whether you are making a spell or just want to use some herbs, some consideration should be given to how you are going to do it.

Amulet - Also called a sachet. Herbs can be carried around or placed in the house and should be put in a small bag, bought or made. Voile bags are ideal. Place a tablespoon of herbs in the bag, you can also add additional items like crystals if you wish. Replace after three months.

Bathing - You can use a cheesecloth sachet for this and include a half to a full cup of herbs. Drop into a warm bath and leave in while you bathe.

Incense -Why not make your own instead of buying incense sticks, it works much better and you can infuse with your own passion and needs while making it. Mix appropriate herbs and resins together and burn as necessary, you will need to use charcoal discs if adding resin and woods.

Infusion - Do not use a metal pan. Keep the herbs covered while infusing so that the steam isn't lost. Use one tsp of herbs to each half mug or a full china tea cup of water. Heat the water until just boiling. Pour over the herb(s) and cover with a lid, let steep for around ten mins.

Strain and cool before use. Infusions can be drunk, used in the bath, sprayed/rubbed onto furniture and floors and used to anoint the body.

Infused oil - This is an oil that has been infused with the properties of one or more herbs. They can be rubbed on the body or used as a base for a salve, also for anointing candles and other altar items. Roots, barks and fresh fragile plants are better used in a heat infusion, as the cold infusion process takes longer. Infused oils can be made from fresh or dried herbs.

Ointments - Any fatty solution to which herbs can be added, lard, petroleum jelly, cocoa butter and add beeswax to make it more solid if you wish. Simply melt what base you are using over a low heat, add the herbs and let steep for around nine minutes. Strain and allow to cool before use. Most powerful when applied to the pulse points. Keep in an airtight container and cool place. Recycled individual preserve jars are ideal

Poppets - Are dolls made to represent a person or animal. They are most often used to spread healing as well as draw money or love. You can also make a poppet to represent yourself.

Placing - Place small amounts of herbs around your home to remove negative energies, offer protection, bring happiness, bring peace etc. Like hanging a garland of marigold above your door to keep negativity out, replace after three months.

Poultice - Usually used for medical purposes. Put your herb into a food processor or blitzer, add a little water to make a thick paste. Spread on your body, ie over your heart if you want to attract love, over your knee if you suffer from arthritis etc. Cover with clean gauze to keep it intact. Change at least once a day.

Salve or Balm - A mixture of soft oils and hardeners such as petroleum jelly or beeswax. You will need to make or buy an herb oil in whatever you want to use.

Scrying - Most people scry into a crystal ball or water, but it is just as easy to use a flame and you can add herbs to the fire to direct your visions. This needs to be done after dark.

Smudging - This is a way to burn herbs to cleanse the body, area or house. A smudge stick is a bundle of herbs, commonly white sage, but you can make your own to fit your own specification, using herbs from the garden.

Chapter 6

Simple Herbal Concoctions

Tranquility Herbal bag - Mix any three of these herbs together:- Jasmine flowers, Bay leaves, Lavender, Rose petals or Rosemary. Fill the herbal mix with your intention while stirring them together. When you feel they are thoroughly mixed and infused with your magic, place them in a voile bag, or similar. You could make a bag from natural material and infuse that with magic too as you make it. Hang the bag in the room your family spends the most time in, to ensure peace and calm.

Banishing powder for doors and windows - Blend together egg shell, black peppercorns, cayenne pepper and cinnamon, with black salt in your pestle and mortar, Blend until nearly a powder. Spend this time envisaging the powder banishing all negativity when it is used. Bottle in an airtight jar and use when required by sprinkling along doorways and window sills. Ideal when unwanted and troublesome guests are coming round!

Handfasting confetti - Mix any four of these herbs:- Cardamom, Clover, Hawthorn wood, Ivy, Marshmallow, Mistletoe or Yarrow. Infuse with love and lasting while you mix them before placing in a cotton or voile bag for safe keeping. After the handfasting ceremony,throw the herbs as you would confetti, knowing that your magical blend is perfectly natural and good for the Earth.

Sleep Blend - Sleep herbs can be used in many different ways. Try mixing Chamomile, lavender and Peppermint into a tea and sip thirty mins before bed.

Alternatively make an incense to burn in the bedroom an hour before retiring for the night, using any 4 of these herbs:- Agrimony, Chamomile, Lavender, Meadowsweet, Peppermint, Raspberry Leaf, Tansy, Valerian, Witches Grass.

Or why not cut Chamomile, Lavender, Valerian and Peppermint fresh from the garden. Use three stems of each herb and tie them together tightly with string or cotton to make a lovely smelling smudge stick or incense stick. You don't even have to burn it, just hang near the bed.

Faery Magic Meditation - Make a beautiful loose incense by mixing three or four of these herbs:- Evening Primrose, Hawthorn Wood, Horsetail, Lady's Mantle, Rowan Berry, Sheep Sorrel or Witches Grass. Burn on a charcoal disc while meditating to increase the chance of the Fae coming around you.

Calming bath blend - Although mixing Elderflower, Patchouli and Peppermint would be my three "go to" herbs for this blend, you can pick any three or four from this list:- Colt's Foot, Borage, Elderflower, Elderberry, Heart's Ease, Patchouli, Peppermint, Penny Royal, Valerian, White Willow. All natural calming herbs, just either sprinkle in your warm bath and leave to infuse with the water or, if your like me and don't like to scrape the dried on herbs off the side of bath later in the day, place them in a piece of fabric, a tea bag or voile bag and tie around the tap so the water flows through the herbs as the bath fills.

Cooking with herbs - If you are cooking a meal, why not consider the herbs you would normally use? While preparing, think about what you want to achieve, be methodical and calm, imbuing your intent as you go. Make sure you make notes as you work, as you may need to make another batch at a later date! While stirring the pan, I envisage the pan as my cauldron and the magic becomes more and more established as I stir. When the meal is ready, you may want to say a few words as a blessing, something like "I ask the God/Goddess to help me bless this food filled with magic and that my desire comes forward with no harm to me or another. So mote it be." Easy herbs to incorporate into everyday food are:- Basil for wealth and protection, Sage for healing, protection and cleansing, Bay leaf for success, strength and wisdom, Peppercorns for banishing, protection and inner strength, Cinnamon for healing, success and luck.

Magical Poultice - Usually made for medical purposes, but very easy to do and kids love them. Finely chop your herbs, add enough water to make a thick paste, spread over the affected area you want to treat and cover with a clean piece of gauze and bandage to keep in place. If you need more than one, change after four hours or when it dries out. Lemon balm grows easily everywhere and is brilliant for small wounds, cold sores and bites, you can place a small amount on the cotton part of a plaster for a child. Other remedies you might like:- Comfrey for sprains and bruises, Rose is great for love issues, a broken heart etc and place the poultice on the heart. Cayenne Pepper for arthritis and bread & milk for infections and boils. Heat the milk and then add bread, use the mix while still hot.

Chapter 7

Making magic simple

Whether you are a witch of 2 days or many generations it doesn't distract from the point we are all very busy people, so by having things to hand or ready made it means you can still do magic, even when you don't have much time. .

Make some small bottles of pre-prepare oils, or sealed bags of mixed incense that meets the needs of your go to spell.

Goddess Anointing Oil - Ideal for anointing candles or any altar items when you don't have time to do a full ceremonial ritual.

Add a pinch of patchouli, frankincense resin, dried rose petals and either sage or lavender to a light carrier oil such as rosehip, almond or grapeseed. Place outside in the full moon energy once made.

Protection Oil - Having ready made protection oil allows you to rub the oil into a candle and perform a very simple candle spell or to rub into your chakra points if it is you who needs the protection.

Add a pinch of galangal, peppermint, goat's rue and vervain, add to a small bottle of light oil, such as rapeseed, grapeseed or almond oil, turn the bottle two or three times a day for 7 days before using, then gently shake the bottle just before each use.

Divination Tea - Mix your dried herbs together and keep in an airtight container with a good label on it, this means when you are in a hurry, you only need to spoon some out of the tub and straight into the strainer.

Use a spoon of any of these herbs to a max of four. Calendula, clove, dandelion root, hibiscus, orange peel or flower, sweet cicely or yarrow.

Sabbat Incense - I like to make my blend up and store in airtight containers, try this easy **Samhain** Incense.

Mix a blend of any four of these herbs and resins. Dried apple, frankincense resin, myrrh resin, pumpkin seeds, rosemary, sage, sandalwood and marigold.

Always be prepared may be the boy scouts motto, but it works really well for witches too. If you feel rushed you're less likely to perform the spell.

"In this day and age preparation is key"

We are all busy people, working, keeping a home, cooking and loving a family, so anything that helps you find that extra10 minutes when you need it has to be good.

Chapter 8

Keeping a record

One of the key aspects of being a successful witch is introspection. This can only be done if you keep a record of your work, thoughts and rituals, where you were, are now and hope to be in the future. If you aren't keeping a record, now is the time to start.

Have as much fun with magic as you want, but always make sure you keep a record of what you do when working magically, so whether you want to call your record keeping a Book of Shadows or just a journal or note pad, it is up to you, of course there is a difference. But how annoying if you make something, it works fabulously and when you need it again a few weeks later, you can't remember what you used!!

A journal is a place to write about your day, events in your life, how you feel, think and what is different today than yesterday. This is your "diary" and is to be read by no one but you. Try to make a commitment to write in the journal every single day. The act of journaling can be life changing.

You may also need or want a magical record. Some people may buy a beautiful leather book and scribe all its contents in ink. Some may use reporters ring bound pads, cheap and easy to replace if you make too many mistakes and some may choose a simple annual diary. Of course more and more people are opting for the online book of shadows now, where everything you need can be stored on the cloud with one simple finger movement.

Personally I love the feel of a good leather bound book, of using a fine ink and quill to keep what amounts to a story of my magical life. My book has little envelopes stuck in it, with recipes written on, pictures, spells written on scraps of paper, old pieces of ripped cardboard, it even has a miniature bottle of protection salt glued in it. The important thing is that all my hard work is stored.

Many of my students ask me where they should start when they first buy their dream book and the only answer I can give is - "wherever you feel like". A book of shadows is very personal, so only you know how you want to start it. The most important thing is that you **do** start it. So many witches tell me they bought a book years before, but continue to store their work in a safe place or a drawer or shoe box because they are frightened to make a mistake in such an important book.

My reply to that is very simple - Witchcraft is a path, you learn constantly, you change your techniques, alter your direction from time to time and advance in fits and starts, so of course you will make mistakes, few people write a spell from scratch and find out it works perfectly first time, a spell often needs tweaking, changing the day you do it on, or one of the herbs you've used, or a sentence here and there. But this is how we learn and what turns us from a new witchling into a fully fledged witch.

Don't be afraid to show your mistakes, they are still a part of you and just as important as the finished article.

Book of Shadows - Where you place all magical workings, ritual work, meditations, spells you've written and over the years the book will get bigger and bigger. This book is for your eyes only and traditionally is burnt with your body when you die.

Grimoire - Where you place all the information that you want to pass down to your children if they are to become hereditary witches. The Grimoire will have go to spells you know will work, sabbat rituals, herbs that are a must, opening and closing circles, altar items. Everything they need to know to continue on the path you have provided. It is a reference to magic for others in the family to follow with your own traditions inside.

Well that is it from me for now. I hope you enjoy using herbs and plants, keeping a record, making lotions and potions and just spending more time in a magical state of mind.

Till next time,

Blessed Be x

Louise

Chapter 9

Journal

The best way to learn is to keep a journal of everything you do, you never know when you may need to recap, so while you are looking for your book of shadows, why not keep your notes in here. Record everything whether it works or not, how else will you learn?

Date:

Notes:

Outcome:

*Date:*_____

Notes:
_____
_____
_____
_____
_____
_____
_____

Outcome:
_____
_____
_____
_____
_____
_____
_____

_____
_____
_____
_____
_____
_____

Date: _____

Notes:

_____
_____
_____
_____
_____
_____

Outcome:

_____
_____
_____
_____
_____
_____

_____
_____
_____
_____
_____

Date: _____

Notes:

_____
_____
_____
_____
_____
_____
_____

Outcome:

_____
_____
_____
_____
_____
_____
_____

_____
_____
_____
_____
_____
_____

Date: _____

Notes:

Outcome:

Date: _____

Notes:

Outcome:

Date:

Notes:

Outcome:

Date: _____

Notes:

Outcome:

Date:

Notes:

Outcome:

Date: _____

Notes:

Outcome:

Chapter 10

Conclude

I really hope you have enjoyed this snippet into witchcraft and the differences between wicca and hedgewitchery. There is of course many other forms of witchcraft and paganism you can follow if this doesn't quite feel "your cup of tea"

Why not try out one of my courses and find out a bit more, most courses are taught in person or via the internet depending on where you live and what is practical for you.

Wicca – What's it all about?

This course comes in three levels and covers all the aspects a beginner needs to know, from what a sabbat is to what you need on your altar and how to do rituals. Great fun and you'll leave with a good bag of things you've made too.

Spellcasting.

Find out how to write spells, cast them and stay safe. What other ways can we create magic and how these other forms of spell casting work. Discuss chanting, circle casting and discharging a spell that is no longer needed.

Reiki – Levels 1, 2 & Masters

Learn Usui Tibetan healing. You will be attuned and taught this system of reiki. Level 1 includes methods for self healing. Level 2 includes distance healing and increasing your abilities and level 3 includes advanced reiki, how to teach and psychic surgery. During the course you will give and receive healing. This is a certified course which will allow you to get insurance.

Hedgewitch 101

The complete beginners course discusses what being a hedgewitch entails and the differences to other forms of witchcraft. Meditation and trance work, elements and elementals and how to connect with them and of course nature, forest bathing and herbs.

Magical Herbalism

Look at 100's of herbs and their magical meanings. How herbs fit into witchcraft. How to grow, dry and store the herbs yourself. Remedies and household products the old way and of course we wouldn't miss out edible and toxic herbs.

Crystal Therapy & Chakra Balancing

Choosing crystals once you know what they are and where they came from. Aura work and exercises and how to ground safely. Work with a dowser and discuss cleaning and charging your crystals, chakra balancing and self treatments. On this course you will give and receive a treatment.

Kitchen Witch – Level 1 & 2

Level 1 looks at what a kitchen witch actually is and does. Food correspondences and how to make environmentally safe household products. Discuss how to stock your spell box by making your own incense, smudge sticks protection salts. What plants and herbs to choose and how to turn a normal Monday night meal into a magical delight.

Level 2 looks at items you might need and how to make a magical first aid box, treatments and poultices. Discuss and take part in Goddess connection meditations and find out who to work with depending on the season or sabbat.

Psychic and Spiritual Development

This is a one day course with a month interval between each level. You will learn about meditation, how to connect to spirit, recognising your own abilities, 6th sense, grounding exercises, Who your spirit guide is? connecting to aura and aura drawing and working with different psychic tools such as Tarot, scrying, psychometry, dowsing and spiritual writing among other exercises and fun tests.

New courses coming shortly include Sacred Trees and Foraging. Keep a lookout on the website for dates.

www.thewiccanlady.co.uk/courses

Printed in Great Britain
by Amazon

65831830R00064